Chapter One

Making

The

Cut?

As an employee working for an enterprise or corporation, the thought may have crossed your mind quite a few times to become your own boss, or at this time you may have already made-up your mind to quit your job.

However, as simple as it sounds, the path of being an entrepreneur is full of uncertainties that involve tough, hard, and quick decision-making, risk-taking and character-testing.

So before taking this path, you should consider these things, which will play an intricate role in your success as an entrepreneur.

ASK YOURSELF

Now let's take a few things into consideration before we even go any further.

Can we be candid?! Answer the following as openly and honestly as possible.

Do you believe wholeheartedly that you have what it takes to go solo?

_____
_____
_____

Are you the kind of individual who will succeed working on their own, each and every day, without supervision?

_____
_____
_____

Will you commit to making personal sacrifices of your time and social activities to put in long days and even longer nights to ensure the success of your business?

_____
_____
_____

Do you have the character, attitude and discipline to manage your day to day business operations without supervision?

_____
_____
_____

IT'S YOUR MOVE

The idea of becoming your own boss is absolutely thrilling and liberating, but it can also be intimidating and, at times, overwhelming; being your own boss will also demand high levels of sacrifice and commitment and will require you to consistently perform at your very best. Every position you take and decision you make will play an intricate detail in the end result of the success of your business.

There will be moments where you indeed will question your decision and judgment of becoming your own boss. These thoughts are likely to surface most often in the times where you are not getting the results you're expecting and desire for your business.

At times there may be feelings of anger, confusion, and lack of confidence, which will only aggravate your thoughts more and add to it doubts about you being wrong in the first place about quitting your stable job and becoming your own boss.

However, it is my belief that where there is doubt, there is destiny; where there is anticipation, there will surely come affirmation. Confirming and reminding you that against all odds, and despite the situations and circumstances, if YOU believe in yourself and your talents, abilities, and capabilities, you can succeed as an entrepreneur!

Now, before leaving your job and taking the leap to becoming your own boss, you must make sure that you have carefully thought through and planned a strategy that will guide you into the opportunity to both leave your job and start your own business.

You must remember that, while taking into consideration the advice and opinions of family and friends who know you well will not hurt anything, it will ultimately be your determination, perseverance, and will power that will ultimately determine if you are cut out to be your own boss.

A crucial component to consider in terms of becoming your own boss is to engage in some meticulous self-searching and determining your own personality and character. Ask yourself, "Would I want a boss like me? What is it about being my own boss that motivates me? How well do I adjust to change?" These are a few things that will assist you along the way because they all are absolutely critical to your success as a business owner. More importantly, you must also be absolutely sure that you are in this for the long term because the truth is, there are going to be lots of long days and even longer nights!

THINGS TO CONSIDER

Here are few things that you might want to consider before making your final decision:

◎ Be practically honest with yourself and diligently seek to determine whether or not you have the right persona and character to make it as your own boss.

◎ Make sure you have adequate skill sets in the specific area of business in which you are looking to develop. If it is determined that you need to acquire additional skill sets, then you should effectively lay out a plan as to how and when you are going to acquire these. Failure to plan is planning to fail.

◎ Get support whether it's in the form of technical, logistics, or mentoring. You will need to consult with those that have been there and done that and could potentially assist you in your endeavor. Don't sell yourself short trying to do it all by yourself!

◉ Find out your work related strengths and weaknesses and emphasize those areas in which you need to improve. Quickly, take the necessary steps needed to develop in these areas.

◉ Manage and fine-tune your key personality traits and recognize who you are and who you want to be, so that you have no problem implementing your ideas and decisions successfully.

◉ To have a successful transition from employee to employer, discovering your aptitude and talent and fine tuning it to its highest level is absolutely essential.

Making the decision to be your own boss is one thing, but recognizing your true potential is the beginning of this process.

Chapter Two

Profession

While a job in the corporate realm brings financial stability, quite often you find yourself stuck in the day-in and day-out process of something you simply do not enjoy doing. You feel like your creative side is dying every day along with the undying fear of being stuck at your current job forever.

Nonetheless, even with these thoughts and fears surfacing, some of us continue to stick in the "I'm just doing this for a paycheck" mindset instead of taking the necessary measures to pursue our lifelong passion.

The thing is this: most dream of this every day, but a few ever do anything about it.

I've found that the main reason only a select few pursue their true passion is that most people are uncertain that their passion would actually yield them a stable career and give them the financial freedom they're hoping for, or more over, most are simply afraid that this desire to profit from their passion just will not work for them.

Operating a business and being your own boss is not simple. It's also not impossible to turn your passion into your profession. The fact is you must be sure of what your passion is.

Each person possesses a unique talent and is good at something. You must take some time to explore your passion and dreams and get a clear vision on what it is that you are passionate about.

It's important to note the fact that once your passion becomes your profession, it's no longer your hobby, it's your career!

PASSIONS' EARNING POTENTIAL

If you can anticipate your passion can be transformed into earning's and can realistically give you a stable career, then it is worth trying to pursue this path.

Here are few pointers that will help you decide the sustainability and earning potential of your passion:

Have you tested the true market potential of your passion?

_____
_____
_____

Does your passion have the appeal so that people can share it and will be willing to pay for it?

_____
_____
_____

Does your passion create a viable product that people will want to buy?

_____
_____
_____

Does your passion create anything unique?

_____
_____
_____

Before making any decisions regarding turning your passion into your profession, you must have a detailed realization of the results that your passion can deliver.

You should do thorough research using all the available resources you can to map out a clear picture of the market opportunities for your passion and its true market potential. You must have a crystal clear vision of how the transformation of your passion into a stable career will happen. Ensure that it is realistic and practical, and you must decide a timeframe for accomplishing this transformation. You must monitor your progress and measure your results continuously.

TRANSITIONING

To pursue your passion you do not have to make the jump to becoming your own boss and changing your career instantly. For starters, you can try to operate as your own employer in a familiar sector and gradually make the transition into setting up a business focused on your passion and get the feel of what its likes to be your own boss.

You must give yourself ample amount of time to properly research and analyze every facet of the needs of your business before you launch it and open up for business.

When someone asks you, "So what is it that you do?" If your reply is, "I am my own boss," the feeling that surfaces with this reply is unexplainable, right? Yes, I know. I've been there.

It has been my experience that it is most employees' dream to become an entrepreneur or at least an executive leader where they ultimately are their own boss (so to say). Entrepreneurship is the epitome of someone's ability to take control of their career. It gives you an opportunity to pursue long-held interests or passions.

Along with the pride and reputation come a number of responsibilities, among the most important of which is leadership. As a leader it's your responsibility to set the path for your company, inspiring employees to do their best and actively taking care of every situation—bad or worse.

You can't assign this responsibility to anybody, nor can you leave things as is, allowing things to hopefully work themselves out. You must always be ready to make decisions that are in the best interest of your business, customers, clients, and employees.

Now when we talk about a boss versus a leader, it should be noted that there is a very fine line between a compassionate leader and a strict boss, so if you aspire to become your own boss and want to run your business smoothly, you need to make a big decision about whether you will be a boss or a leader. You want to be a boss who sets the standards and guidelines for employees so that they are as productive as possible.

Every leader can be a boss, but not every boss can be leader! So if you aspire to become your own boss and want to run your business ethically, with morals, and demonstrated leadership, you should first understand that there is a difference between a boss and a leader.

As a leader you want to set the standards high by leading with definition, and integrity versus acting only as a boss dictating, delegating and pushing guidelines for employees to follow.

Now don't get me wrong a leader definitely is a delegator, dictator, and process overseer; however, let it be noted that in this capacity, a leader has already mastered the understanding that it is imperative that the first act as a leader is to lead by example, in morals, ethics and character. Often times, a boss is not concerned about these things—only your ability to get the job done.

Here are few things you can consider that will help decide how effective you are as a leader or if your entrepreneur characteristic is that of a boss:

◉ Do you frequently supervise economic and social trends that affect your employees, customers, team members, and others?

◉ Do you encourage employees, team members, and others whom you may have the ability to influence their decision or thought process as it relates to how they may carry out a specific task to be more creative or assume more responsibility?

◉ In the times of crucial conversations or workplace conflict, do you work with employees, team members, and others on understanding how and why it happened, rather than holding them responsible without listening to any facts?

◉ Do your company's policies reflect flexibility and consideration of various needs?

◉ Do you have a real-time communication with employees, team members, and others you encounter in the workplace? And do you encourage them to have open communication with you on regular basis?

In the world of entrepreneurship and small business, there is a constant state of change, and any business who wants to continue to stay in business must adapt to these changes. Besides keeping the duplex form of communication with your employees, a leader or boss is required to have a collaborative dialogue with business owners in their specific industry. They are required to discover ideas that can be implemented to their own business, as well as recent developments that can motivate and help to retain their present employees.

It is a process where you gain experience by learning new things each and every day and improves your chances of becoming a successful leader.

Being a good leader or boss takes effort and dedication! You will spend lots of time every day working and perfecting your business module.

There are lots of resources, books, and coaches available that can guide you and work with you in this process... You must take note that it is inherently important for you to accept honest and constructive criticism. It will give you direction on where and when you require fine tuning in your decision making approach.

Lead with conviction! Know your values, not just opinions, but the principles that guide your decision making every day especially where matters of integrity are involved.

Chapter Four

Finance

The biggest and most important factor that will decide your success with becoming your own boss is how well you can manage your finances. How effective are you in managing the cash flow? When you have a job, you know that there will be a fixed salary and when it will be deposited into your bank account. Operating your own business means that you will not receive any pre-established income to spend. There is no such certainty, and monthly expenditures may well exceed what you earn.

It is a constant fact that running a business is a roller coaster ride in terms of earnings.

The thing with starting a businesses is, even after putting the initial investment required for start-up, there will be no income until you find customers and they have decided to pay you. You must accept this rule of business: customers are in no hurry to do pay you upfront! In due course, your business will establish into a pattern, and you will be enlightened with the financial wisdom over the time to predict your earnings, expenditure, and seasonal fluctuations.

Becoming your own boss and opening your dream business is a major accomplishment. However exciting this idea might look on paper, to execute it on the ground will take an immense amount of dedication, time, work, and money. Now, to keep the momentum going, you must be aware of the business principles contained in this chapter.

UNDERSTAND BASIC ACCOUNTING

One can be skilled and talented as a Restaurateur, Baker, Designer, or Architect, but if one doesn't know basic accounting tools and doesn't dynamically involve with the cash flow management of their business enterprise, they might not see the light on the other side of the tunnel.

It is important to have the knowledge of the financial side of managing a business relative to your product and service development. You must not exclusively trust professionals for doing all of your financial paperwork; you must have the real-time knowledge of your money. You must review your company's balance sheet regularly, which will give you an idea of your earnings and expenditure. You should never ignore our business's business.

BUSINESS AND PERSONAL EXPENSES

The basic rule of business is to keep personal finances and business finances absolutely separate, because combining them both will produce tax, liability and accounting problems. To offset the desire to mix finances, you must also give preference to your personal budget which is as important as your business budget. Don't get carried away because you anticipate profits coming in the future. Do not spend what you do not have.

PAY YOUR TAXES

To be a successful business owner, paying income taxes regularly is must and is one of the toughest phases of being self-employed. Take an active role in tax paying process and try to cover all your vulnerabilities.

THE TOTAL

Establishing your new business' finances in order is the most imperative responsibility that requires your full focus and will test your skill and knowledge so that you can quantify your honest work into some cash.

Chapter Five
Family

There may be various pros of becoming your own boss but also some cons you can't neglect. There are few personal sacrifices to be made to achieve success. Starting up and running your own business is not a regular pay job but involves working long hours which impacts the personal lives of entrepreneurs. But the coin has a flip side too. The life of an entrepreneur by default has vulnerabilities which can unbalance the work/life equilibrium.

PREPARATION

When one takes the leap and starts a new business the entire family is affected and it demands their involvement in implicit way. Becoming an entrepreneur can be emotionally challenging and time consuming. The difficulties and tough situation can have a psychological impact on you and your family. This problem can intensify when family members don't show support or even resent the idea of the new business.

This is why it becomes essential for any entrepreneur to draw a line between professional and family life; in this way you and your family will mutually give the respect, support, and trust to each other.

It's your responsibility before you take the high road and fly solo, to prepare your family for the entrepreneurial path. Your spouse and your children deserve to be engaged from the start in the process about what's involved with the transition from having a job to running a business.

BUILDING RELATIONSHIPS

According to Brad Feld and Amy Batchelor in their book *Startup Life: Surviving and Thriving in a Relationship with an Entrepreneur,* it is tough to build a startup company, but it also tough enough to maintain a lasting relationship.

To successfully come out a winner by countering these challenges, you need to be fully aware of the importance of communication, expectations, and shared values. In their book, they mention strategies like "four minutes in the morning" and Life Dinners. Brad and Amy have laid a foundation for communication that helps entrepreneurs manage their busy lives.

BALANCE

The important aspect a successful entrepreneur requires is flexibility to maintain a work/life balance. You can never ascertain the uncertainty the next day is likely going to throw at you. When you start your own business, then you must prepare yourself, from the beginning, for carrying out a number of jobs, fulfilling the responsibilities to which you are accountable for, and keeping the balance between family and work.

You must remember that just like scheduling your work works for you, scheduling your life is what that will keep balance between your personal and professional life. You must give time to activities like daily exercise with family, a weekly date or social night, asking kids about their studies and personal life, and a yearly vacation.

Maintaining a steady work and personal life is an important aspect for becoming a successful entrepreneur. Making the best use of your time through effective time management and building in personal/family time into your schedule will help to maintain a healthy work-life balance.

In Conclusion, making the transition from employee to employer can be very rewarding, especially if this decision is derived from the fact that you're seeking your passion! What an exciting and liberating feeling and sense of accomplishment it is!

Working in my passion has helped me discover my purpose and has given me a sense of freedom and liberation that I would not have experienced otherwise working for 40+ years for a corporation.

While I had to take many things into consideration that I've shared with you in this study guide, I can say that I made the best decision in pursuing a personal happiness that gives me an immeasurable peace of mind.

If you are contemplating the decision to leave your job and pursue your passion and desires to become your own employer, I encourage you to take the leap. That desire that's burning inside of you will not go away. You will ultimately become miserable in your day to day as an employee, lacking productivity and no longer a viable resource to the company in which you are working for. However, transitioning responsibly is key. You must be honest with yourself about yourself and your ability to be disciplined enough to be your own boss. You must seek for continuous growth and development opportunities as you venture out into this new path.

Most importantly remember what drove your decision to leave your job and become your own boss because there will be times when you will for sure question that decision.

However, when you make the decision to do what you LOVE, you LOVE what you do, and it will always motivate you to keep going!

Wishing you well in your transition,

~Trisha Love

www.ingramcontent.com/pod-product-compliance
Lightning Source LLC
Chambersburg PA
CBHW061234180526
45170CB00003B/1289